Annual 2011

Posy Edwards

Introduction

The four London lads who won our hearts on *The X Factor*, Aston, Marvin, JB and Oritsé have come a long way since their first dose of life in pop. They might have lost in the 2008 final, but the group have gone on to become the most successful group ever to graduate from the show. They've had hit singles, a number one album, they've wowed thousands of fans on sell-out headline tours, won MOBOs and BRITs – and now they've caught the attention of global sensations like Rihanna and her mentor, the mighty Jay-Z!

You might have seen them on screen – but do you know what aftershave each member likes to wear, or what they asked for last Christmas? Find out what they really look for in a girl, as well as their own favourite music, films and books. Discover all the behind-the-scenes gossip, as well as fun activities, including styling your own JLS dance routine!

chapter 1

hello boys!

You know them as JLS – now meet Aston, Marvin, JB and Oritsé! These gorgeous boys have become the biggest boyband of the year, have stormed the charts with their catchy songs, cute smiles and their amazing dance moves and yet have still managed to keep both feet on the ground. How do they do it? Let's find out . . .

spotlight on ASTON

NAME – Aston Merrygold

BIRTHDAY – 13th February 1988

YOUR FIRST KISS OR CRUSH – The Olsen twins (still to this day)

FIRST (OR WORST) JOB – Shop assistant

FAVOURITE BOOK – Lewis Hamilton's

BROTHERS AND SISTERS? – One sister, five brothers

TATTOOS – One on his back (music symbol)

FAVOURITE SHOP – All Saints and Topman

DO YOU PLAY ANY INSTRUMENTS? – No, but want to learn and will!

WHAT MAKES YOU LAUGH? – A lot of things, even things I shouldn't laugh at (whoops!)

IDEAL DATE? (WHERE, AND WHO?) – On a beach (romantic, I know) with . . . there's too many of them to choose from!!

FAVOURITE TV SHOW – *The Simpsons*

EMBARRASSING SECRET – His prize possession is a *Sonic The Hedgehog* cuddly toy which he asks his mum to look after at home when he's away on tour. What a softy!

HIS PERFECT NEW YEAR'S CELEBRATION – A low key one! In 2009, sweetheart Aston took his mum and dad out for dinner at Gilgamesh in Camden

ASTON'S IRRITATING HABIT – He has too much energy. Sometimes when the boys are all in a car together, Aston gets on their nerves!

To celebrate
winning the MOBOs,
Aston bought
an Audi TT!

To celebrate winning the MOBOs, Marvin also bought an Audi TT! 'As I drove it home, I thought, "Wow, this is all because of JLS."'

NAME – Marvin Humes

BIRTHDAY – 18th March 1985

BIRTHPLACE – Greenwich, London

BROTHERS AND SISTERS – Yes, Leon & Jackson

FIRST CRUSH? – Pamela Anderson in Baywatch!

IDEAL DATE? (WHERE, AND WHO?) – Gilgamesh in Camden with Cheryl Cole!

WHAT IS YOUR BIGGEST AMBITION FOR THE FUTURE? – To have an amazing family!

FAVOURITE RECENT ALBUMS – Maxwell's *BLACKsummers'night*, Jay-Z's *The Blueprint 3*, Cheryl Cole's *3 Words* and Alexandra Burke's *Overcome*

MARVIN'S HOME SECRETS – Marvin and Aston live together, but they don't drive each other mad – they love living together! 'We get on really well. We are all like brothers – closer than brothers. Those three boys I know more than anyone else in my life. We are having the time of our lives, every day with each other just having the biggest laughs.'

spotlight on
JB

NAME – Jonathan Benjamin Gill

BIRTHDAY – 7th December 1986

BROTHERS AND SISTERS – One brother

TATTOOS – None

IDEAL DATE? (WHERE, AND WHO?) – Megan Fox in Cuba!

WHAT IS YOUR BIGGEST AMBITION FOR THE FUTURE? – To retire at 35

WHAT WAS YOUR WORST JOB? – Doing admin at his mum's office. 'It's boring, but it pays the bills!'

JB'S PARTY TRICK – The Carlton dance (by Carlton from *Fresh Prince of Bel Air*)

BIGGEST CELEBRITY CRUSH – Alicia Keys. 'She's incredible – amazing voice, incredible writing talents and she's such a good performer. She's cute too!'

JB DOESN'T GET STAR-STUCK – 'We have to work in this industry so, although I admire what people have achieved, it's about getting the job done.'

HE THINKS A GOOD EDUCATION IS REALLY IMPORTANT – 'My back-up plan was uni. I was doing theology. It was in case things didn't work out. I could have got a nine-to-five job or gone into journalism or law until I got into songwriting. There are skills you can transfer, like organising your own schedule. You can learn valuable life skills from doing a degree.'

JB'S SECRET – He used to play rugby with Warlingham RFC. He was a key player, and even played for Warlingham and Surrey up to under-18 level.

FAVOURITE MOVIES – *The Godfather* and *Pulp Fiction*

To celebrate winning the MOBOs, JB didn't buy anything . . . the sensible hunk is saving up for a house instead

NAME – Oritsé Williams

BIRTHDAY – 27th November 1986

LIFELONG AMBITION – To be a singer

SCHOOL-TIME BLUES – Boys used to tease Oritsé at primary school because he sang in a choir with girls, while the other boys were out playing football

EARLY BRUSHES WITH FAME – Oritsé was busking on Neal Street in London as a teenager, when Louis Walsh walked past him! Oritsé ran after him and asked if he could sing for him, but Louis was in a rush and didn't have time. But Oritsé obviously made an impression – because when he appeared on *The X Factor*, Louis remembered their early encounter!

CELEBRITY CRUSHES – Oritsé thinks Mel B is sexy as hell, for an older woman – and he thinks Rihanna is the bomb!

To celebrate winning the MOBOs, Oritsé went on a spending spree! 'I spent £1,000 on clothes in one day, including bondage trousers from a punk store – yes, I know it's weird!'

The making of JLS

Unlike many groups that only form to compete in *The X Factor*, JLS actually formed a year before they ended up on the show. Although each individual member of the group was a serious musical talent, they were brought together by Oritsé. Oritsé had the grand plan to start a boy band when he was studying at university in London, way back in 2007. He didn't know anyone who could join the group so he set about the search for three other members.

He spent weeks and weeks pouring over adverts in music magazines and flicking through MySpace pages in search of special talents. But in the end, it was his friends who led him to the boys that ended up in the group's line-up: Aston, Marvin, and JB.

Oritsé met Marvin at Oxford Circus in London. When Marvin auditioned for him right there in the street – singing and dancing on the pavement – Oritsé knew JLS had found its first new member. It was Marvin who recommended Aston to Oritsé. Marvin and Aston had met at an audition for a TV advert, and thought he'd be a perfect addition to the group.

The final member to join was JB. Oritsé had met scores of other potentials, but none of them had that special spark. But the second he met JB, he knew that JB's charisma and charm meant he was the perfect final part to the puzzle.

Although the boys didn't have any intention of competing on *The X Factor*, their friends and families started telling them they should apply. Oritsé was against it at first, adamant that he wanted the band to gain fame the old fashioned way – through sheer hard work and determination. But the boys talked about it and decided to give it a go. They weren't banking on winning it anyway, just thinking they might get some good publicity from taking part. They couldn't have guessed how it would turn out for them.

JACK THE LAD SWING – JLS was a name they came up with as a mixture of their cheeky onstage persona and the US music genre New Jack Swing. 'There were a lot of quality UK solo acts like Lemar and Craig David, but Oritsé had spotted a gap in the market that he wanted to fill. But to do it with a British twist,' says JB.

The JLS Quiz

1. What was the name of the group Marvin was a member of before joining JLS?

  a VR
  b ST
  c AI
  d VS

2. In the video for 'Beat Again', what does the dance choreography revolve around?

  a Lung breaths
  b Heartbeats
  c Brainwaves
  d Fingers snapping

3. In the final of *The X Factor*, JLS performed their own version of 'Hallelujah'. But which other contestant also performed this during the show's run?

  a Eoghan Quigg
  b Alexandra Burke
  c Diana Vickers
  d Rachel Hylton

4. Which judge mentored the boys during their X Factor experience?

  a Louis Walsh
  b Cheryl Cole
  c Simon Cowell
  d Dannii Minogue

5. Which number one single did 'Beat Again' knock off from top spot when it soared up the charts?

  a 'Bulletproof' – La Roux
  b 'Bodies' – Robbie Williams
  c 'Sweet Dreams' – Beyoncé
  d 'Evacuate the Dancefloor' – Cascada

6. Before settling on 'JLS', what name did the boys originally perform under?

  a CEO
  b NONO
  c UFO
  d G2G

7. Which famous celebrity sisters does Aston claim to have a crush on?

  a Hilary and Haylie Duff
  b Kim and Kourtney Kardashian
  c Jessica and Ashlee Simpson
  d Mary-Kate and Ashley Olsen

8. What television drama did Marvin appear on?

  a *Holby City*
  b *The Bill*
  c *Doctor Who*
  d *Hollyoaks*

9. What charity single did JLS join in performing for victims of the Haiti Earthquake?

  a 'Hero'
  b 'Everybody Hurts'
  c 'Feed the World'
  d 'Walk this Way'

10. One of the boy's all time heroes, Jay-Z, has stated that JLS are set to become one of the world's biggest boy bands. Which legendary group did he compare them to?

  a The Osmond Brothers
  b Jackson 5
  c *NSYNC
  d Backstreet Boys

11. Who is the oldest member of JLS?

  a Aston
  b Marvin
  c JB
  d Oritsé

12. What was Aston's nickname before JLS?

  a AM
  b LK
  c Aston
  d Diesel

13. Where is Marvin's scar?

a Right arm
b Left leg
c Tummy
d Back

14. Which band member was auditioned on the outskirts of a football pitch?

a Aston
b Marvin
c JB
d Oritsé

15. What does JB stand for?

a Josh Ben
b Jordan Bobby
c Joker B
d Jonathan Benjamin

16. Who loves tomato ketchup?

a Aston
b Marvin
c JB
d Oritsé

17. What's Aston's number plate on his car?

a Just living life
b One shot
c JLS
d Aston baby

18. Who started the band?

a Aston
b Marvin
c JB
d Oritsé

19. What's Marvin's favourite holiday destination?

a Egypt
b Barbados
c America
d Thailand

20. How did they get their colours?

a Favourite colours
b Manager
c Photographers thought they looked good
d Randomly

For the answers go to page 63

chapter 2

The X Factor and beyond

Even though the boys never thought they'd get far on *The X Factor*, it was pretty clear from the start of the show that they were leagues ahead of the competition. They had already put in thousands of hours working together – singing, dancing, choreographing routines and writing songs. They were a real group with a brotherly bond, and it showed.

Building the dream!

The boys bounce back

Oritsé was shocked at the reception the boys were getting. 'Everyone said to us – from the producers to the judges to the back-stage crew at *The X Factor* – "we can't believe that you're a real group." That was alien to us. We couldn't believe that people would go for it if we weren't.'

JLS ended up being mentor Louis Walsh's last act in the competition after just two weeks, and even though they had some testing moments on the show, they managed to hang in there with strong performances, until they reached the semi-final. The boys seemed to be riding high when disaster struck. JLS had decided to sing Rihanna's hit single 'Umbrella', performing alongside princess RiRi herself. But it wasn't to be. Days before the final, Rihanna cancelled. All the confidence that JLS had suddenly disappeared. They were worried they didn't have enough time to prepare another performance. But they ended up with the most votes in the semi final, and sailed through to face Eoghan Quigg and Alexandra Burke in the final.

The finals!

They survived the first vote of the night (in which Eoghan Quigg was voted off), but were ultimately beaten by finalist Alexandra Burke. Being the polite and gracious group of boys that they are, JLS immediately surrounded Alex and congratulated her on her big win.

Though they were constantly in the presence of so many stars, the boys kept a cool head and didn't allow themselves to get star-struck . . . JB: 'We have to work in this industry so, although I admire what people have achieved, it's about getting the job done'.

JLS Killer Dance Secrets
Learn the Body Pop!

You'll have noticed, no doubt, that JLS have got some killer moves on the dance floor! All accomplished dancers and gymnasts, the boys like to bust out their shapes at any given opportunity. One of their favourite moves is the body pop. Body popping is the basis for nearly all hip hop dances. Once you know the basics you can use them to freestyle in your own individual way – but you've got to get those basics down first!

The most important part when doing a body pop is to only move one single part of your arm at any time. It's important to get the process right. Once you've mastered that, you can build up in speed.

STEP 1 – Start with your right hand palm down about a foot away from your body, in line with the top of your stomach.

STEP 2 – Now bend all your fingers so they're pointing down to the floor, but only as far as your middle knuckle.

STEP 3 – Then you need to drop the rest of your fingers as far as your actual knuckles.

STEP 4 – Then you turn your whole hand down from the wrist, so your whole hand is pointing down. Now at this point, your hand is pointing down to the ground, but you need to make sure that your wrist is positioned so that it is higher than your elbow.

STEP 5 – Now you need to flip up your fingers so that they are pointing up to the sky. You also need to move your elbow up at the same time.

STEP 6 – Lift up your right shoulder, as if you are trying to touch your right ear.

STEP 7 – Now lift up your left shoulder in the same way. As you lift your left shoulder, you need to move your right shoulder down at the same time, so they look like they're swapping positions.

STEP 8 – Move your left shoulder back down. Now you need to copy Step 5, but for your left arm. Your palm needs to be flat, and held out a foot and a half away from your body. Your fingers need to be reaching up towards the sky.

STEP 9 – Then you drop all your fingers so they are pointing to the ground, from your actual knuckles.

STEP 10 – Now you need to bend your fingers so they're only pointing down from your middle knuckles.

STEP 11 – Then you finish with your left hand palm down about a foot away from your body, in line with the top of your stomach.

EASY! ONCE YOU'VE GOT THE BASICS, YOU CAN ADD YOUR OWN INDIVIDUAL STYLE TO THE BODY POP. BY FOLLOWING THESE SIMPLE INSTRUCTIONS, YOU'VE GOT THE START OF YOUR VERY OWN STREET DANCE!

Life after *The X Factor*

After their success on the *The X Factor*, JLS hit the road with *The X Factor* tour, wowing thousands of screaming fans with sharp dance routines and sweet harmonies. There were rumours that Simon Cowell was going to sign the boys to his label, but the deal fell through and JLS ended up in the capable hands of Epic Records, the home of stars like Lemar, Jay-Z, Sean Kingston and even their number one hero, Michael Jackson.

The number 1 spot

The boys worked hard on their debut single, 'Beat Again' which smashed the number one spot in the British charts. After *The X Factor Live* tour was over, the talented foursome were asked to support R'n'B soul star Lemar on tour. Awesome!

On the road

The boys won themselves thousands of new fans on the tour. Their popularity was sky-high – and they even found themselves nominated for the 2009 MOBO Awards. Aston, Marvin, JB and Oritsé were thrilled just to be nominated and they couldn't believe it when they walked out of the awards ceremony with two accolades, for Best Song with 'Beat Again', and Best Newcomer, beating their *X Factor* rival and pal, Alexandra Burke.

They enjoyed more chart success with second single 'Everybody in Love', which went to number one in the UK Charts, knocking Cheryl Cole's single off the top spot. They repeated their success with debut album *JLS*, which knocked Chezza off the top spot again and beat Robbie Williams too. Pretty amazing achievements for the four London lads!

Back in the studio

They had managed to achieve so much in such a short space of time – despite not winning *The X Factor*, the boys were invited back onto the 2009 show to perform as the most successful group ever to graduate from the show. In just two short years, they had made it to the top – as the thousands of screaming fans singing along to their second single 'Everybody in Love' reminded them!

Living the high life

As well as selling thousands of records and having to escape from mobs of fans, the boys were starting to live the celebrity lifestyle with celebrity friends. Nearly a year to the day after their X Factor final, the boys were out celebrating JB's birthday, along with the girls from The Saturdays and former Sugababe Mutya Buena. The Sugababes and The Saturdays – usually rival girl bands when they aren't partying together – also came to help Aston celebrate his 22nd birthday. Lucky boy Aston!

Both feet on the ground

But despite all their celebrity high-life partying, the boys still have their feet on the ground and have their priorities in order. They took a couple of trips to hospitals in London to visit teenage cancer patients. All the boys understand how lucky they are to be in the limelight, and want to use it to help others. 'It's nice to be in a position to do something like this,' says Aston.

'We've had a really lovely afternoon. It's just great to put a smile on people's faces.'

Although the boys are devoted to helping their fans, sometimes the fans get a little too excited and need to be restrained! One of their fans zipped herself into a suitcase to try and go on tour with the boys. A mob of fans turned up to see the boys turn on the Christmas lights in Manchester, and there were so many of them that the entrance was completely blocked, and JLS couldn't actually get into the building!

Drama!

Band member Oritsé was even unintentionally assaulted by a fan who ran up to his car for an autograph. Oritsé wound down the window, but the fan was so excited she accidentally shoved her pen in his face, just missing his eye! She then had to be pulled away by security. Now that sounds like a close call!

Q. What's the craziest thing a fan's done to meet you?
JB: In Glasgow they set off the fire alarm, so everyone had to leave the hotel. They went crazy when they saw us. They're meeting their heroes, which is us, which is a bit weird. They see us as icons so they do whatever they can to meet us.

29

ACROSS

1. What is the name of JLS' first smash hit single?
2. Who is Marvin's ideal date?
3. What can't Aston eat his dinner without?
4. What famous reality TV show did the boys get their lucky break?
5. What American diva has said that JLS are going to be the biggest boyband in the world!?

DOWN

6. What does JLS stand for?
7. What month is JB born in?
8. Finish the line of this JLS song. 'Everybody in…'?
9. Which member of the band formed JLS?
10. How many Brit awards were the boys nominated for in 2009?

JLS Wordsearch

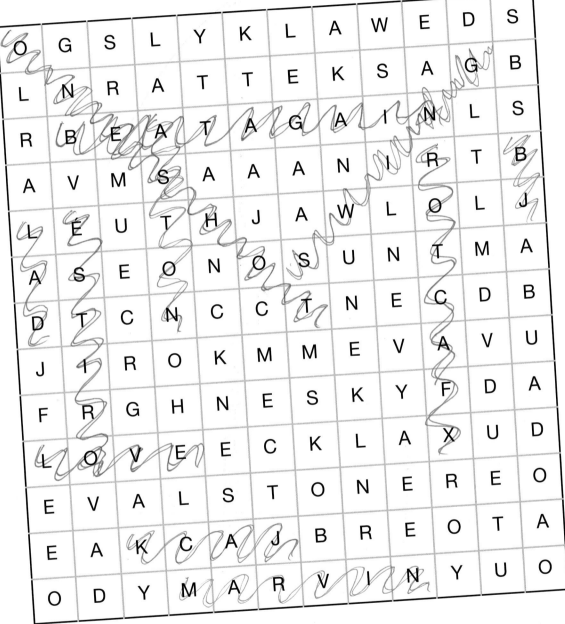

O	G	S	L	Y	K	L	A	W	E	D	S
L	N	R	A	T	T	E	K	S	A	G	B
R	B	E	A	T	A	G	A	I	N	L	S
A	V	M	S	A	A	A	N	I	R	T	B
L	E	U	T	H	J	A	W	L	O	L	J
A	S	E	O	N	O	S	U	N	T	M	A
D	T	C	N	C	C	T	N	E	C	D	B
J	I	R	O	K	M	M	E	V	A	V	U
F	R	G	H	N	E	S	K	Y	F	D	A
L	O	V	E	E	C	K	L	A	X	U	D
E	V	A	L	S	T	O	N	E	R	E	O
E	A	K	C	A	J	B	R	E	O	T	A
O	D	Y	M	A	R	V	I	N	Y	U	O

BEAT AGAIN
ONE SHOT
LOVE
ASTON

MARVIN
ORITSÉ
JB
X FACTOR

JACK
LAD
SWING

Touring time

No sooner was New Year out of the way, than the swoonsome foursome headed off on a tour across the UK. The show was electric, and featured Aston, Marvin, JB and Oritsé ripping off their shirts and dancing their way through a tight set, to the background sound of thousands of girls screaming! As well as singing their own tracks, the boys performed a tribute to one of their all time heroes, Michael Jackson.

But they had to tone down their performances, because some of the venues couldn't cope with everything they had planned! Instead, they decided to save all the flying, pyrotechnics and back-flipping for their BRITs performance and winter arena tour. Amazing!

'We always want to improve, and for me personally I am always striving for the next show to be better than the one before.'
ORITSÉ

Sold out!

The tour was a lot of hard work for JLS, but it was totally sold-out – and a total success! Not satisfied with dancing themselves dizzy, they also started work on their second album while out on the road. Busy boys!

'Performing nearly every night will hopefully inspire something in us for the songs,' says Marvin.

'For us, a song can come from anywhere. We're up for anything and want to enjoy what we're doing.'

It was a hectic and exhausting six weeks, but the boys were sad when it ended. Over 50,000 eager fans tried to win tickets to the last show, but only 3,000 were lucky enough to make it into their final performance. It was an awesome show, and featured a star-studded celebrity audience too – among them, Spice Girl Geri Halliwell, the Saturdays' Rochelle Wiseman, Sugababe Amelle Berrabah, Alan Carr and rapper Tinie Tempah from N-Dubz.

The BRITS

When they thought 2010 couldn't get any better, the soulful group were delighted to hear they had been nominated for three BRIT awards! The nominations were especially important to the group, who had all dreamed of attending the famous BRIT School for Performing Arts as kids.

'We've all grown up watching the show so we'd love to win a BRIT but we can't think about that we've just to go out there and enjoy ourselves', said Marvin.

Summer shows

The band managed a small rest in the spring, but the downtime didn't last long, as they had some summer shows planned as warm-ups before their massive winter arena tour! They strutted their stuff at festivals, but kept very quiet about what fans were going to witness in the arena tour: the only thing they would let slip was that it was going to be JLS – but bigger and better than anyone had ever witnessed before!

In demand!

Although fans were excited by the BRITs and the summer shows, even more exciting was the news that none other than the godfather of the modern urban pop scene, Jay-Z, was interested in working with the boys! Barbadian beauty Rihanna was also excited about collaborating with them. 'Working with JLS is something that will happen this year,' she said. 'Jay will make stars out of them. He has been a great mentor to me. He has been around long enough to spot real talent and he knows who will become worldwide stars. America has only had a little taste of them so far, but give it probably as little as 18 months and they could be the most famous band in the world!'

To make sure the band are on the right track, the group's management drew up a top secret five year strategy, charting the boyband's rise to world domination! The plan allegedly sees the band releasing a new album every November until 2015, followed by an arena tour. As well as that, the boys are definitely working on cracking America.

Sounds exhausting! But as long as the gorgeous boys find the time to come home and perform live for us, we don't mind one bit!

Showbiz is full of temptations. Have you ever taken drugs?
ASTON: No. My dad was a policeman and told me horror stories that put me off for life.
MARVIN: None of us do drugs. If one of us was slipping off the rails, we'd pull him back in.

chapter 3

style

It's no coincidence that the boys are well known for their sharp, colourful outfits. When they first got together, they spent a long time working on their look. Now they're lucky enough to have personal stylists and get clothes sent to them for free!

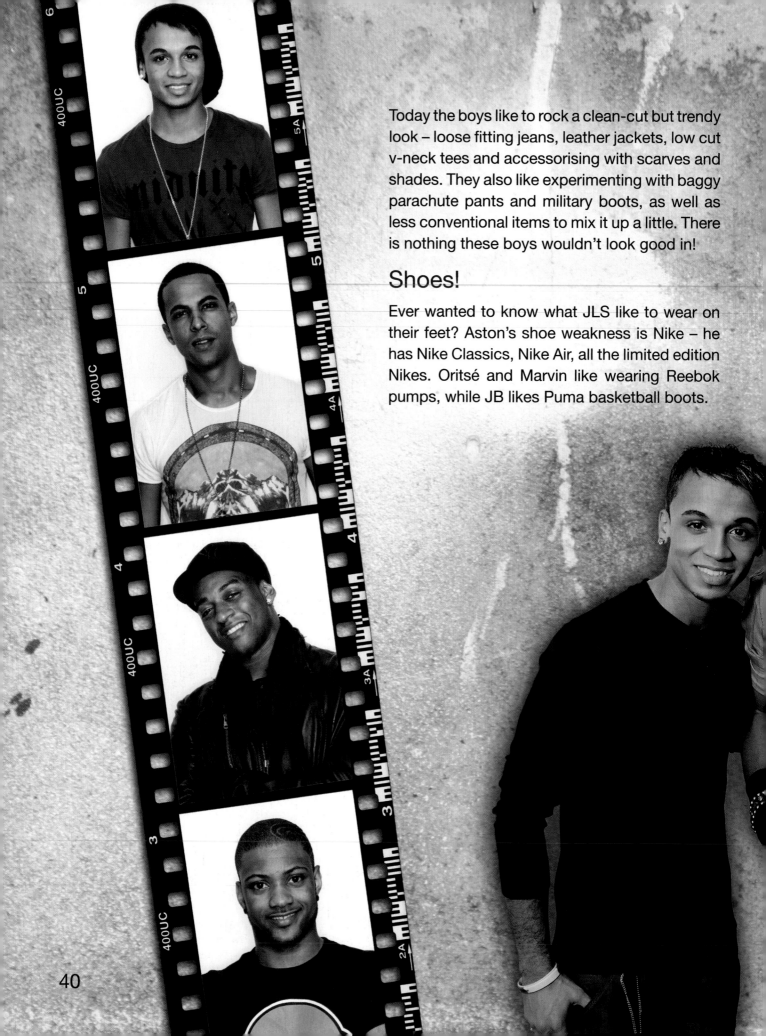

Today the boys like to rock a clean-cut but trendy look – loose fitting jeans, leather jackets, low cut v-neck tees and accessorising with scarves and shades. They also like experimenting with baggy parachute pants and military boots, as well as less conventional items to mix it up a little. There is nothing these boys wouldn't look good in!

Shoes!

Ever wanted to know what JLS like to wear on their feet? Aston's shoe weakness is Nike – he has Nike Classics, Nike Air, all the limited edition Nikes. Oritsé and Marvin like wearing Reebok pumps, while JB likes Puma basketball boots.

Bling bling!

Aston loves to wear watches – the group have their own watches made by LTD, but he also loves G-shock and Black Dice watches. Oritsé prefers wearing New Era hats to wearing jewellery, as does JB. The whole group are totally excited about their own line of jewellery – dog tags that they designed themselves – with all the money going to help underprivileged children in London. Now that's a good cause!

41

JLS Killer Dance Secrets
Learn the Body Wave!

The body wave is a variation of body popping, and it's a move that the boys like to use in the clubs as well as on stage! Instead of going from side to side, the body wave creates the illusion of a wave travelling through your body from top to bottom, and back again.

STEP 1 – Stand with your feet shoulder width apart, with your arms hanging loose at your sides.

STEP 2 – Lift both your shoulders up together, like you're trying to touch your ears.

STEP 3 – Now roll both your shoulders backwards, while pushing your chest out in front of you at the same time.

STEP 4 – Now pull your chest back in, and push your hips forward to make your stomach stick out. Once you're more confident, you can also bring your shoulders forward, which makes the shape stronger.

STEP 5 – Pull your stomach in slightly, and push your hips forward.

STEP 6 – Move your hips back, and then push your knees forward. You do this by going up on tiptoes.

STEP 7 – Now put your heels back on the ground.

STEP 8 – Make your knees straight, and now move your hips forward.

STEP 9 – Move your hips back while pushing your stomach out and forward.

STEP 10 – Pull your stomach back in, and push your chest out.

AND VOILA! THE BODY WAVE IS YOURS!

chapter 4

love and romance

When you're as gorgeous as the members of JLS, it's unsurprising that the rumour mill is off the hook when it comes to romance! All four members of the group have been romantically linked with every hot celebrity they've stood within ten feet of – and some they've never even met!

To keep the fans happy, JLS released their debut album with five different covers, four of which feature an individual member of the band. And the band are having a 'good-natured' competition! 'We are keeping tally!' says Marvin. 'At the moment Aston has sold most with me second, then JB and Oritsé at the bottom!'

People said that Aston was dating glamour model Sophie Houghton but it just wasn't true! 'The thing with this girl, right, is that I have never met her in my life. Never!' he says. 'I don't understand how it became a story. People say these things and it is all completely made up! We were supposed to have met up at the show in Hammersmith and it's not true. And apparently she said we'd met up another time also. Totally not true. I'm single and looking for love.' There's still hope for us then!

In the spotlight

They'll have to have nerves of steel to face down their determined fans though! 'The women are crazy!' laughs JB. 'We have had girls going up and down in a lift for 12 hours trying to catch us in a hotel. Bras and knickers are constantly being thrown on stage. One hit me in the face and I went to pick it up so loads of other girls took theirs off and threw them at us.'

Q. What perfume do you like women to wear?
MARVIN:
I like Dior Poison. That's a sexy smell!

Love is in the air!

Continuing the band's connection with The Saturdays, Marvin recently started dating singer Rochelle Wiseman, who has a birthday the day after his! The two were spotted flirting with each other at an Alicia Keys album launch in December, then went public with their relationship in March 2010. 'She is such a lovely girl. I'm very fond of her,' says Marvin. 'We've been on a couple of dates, and we're going to see how it goes. She is really very lovely. That's all I can say right now,' he said. 'We get on really well together, but it's early days.'

And for the moment, the rest of the group are single, and though they have been seeing girls, there's no-one special out there yet. And if you think that you'd be perfect girlfriend-material for one of the JLS boys, well, you're in luck, because they're happy to date fans! 'Of course, they're just people,' says sensible JB. 'My ex-girlfriend was a fan of the group.' So we still stand a chance girls!

Q. Who is the vainest in the group?
JB: Oritsé. He checks his hair every two minutes. He takes an hour
to get ready. ASTON: He puts a hat on and stares at himself for five
minutes. Imagine a whole outfit! ORITSÉ: I'm into how I look. I want
to represent my personality – extravagant and colourful

Do you know which of the boys is an Aquarius, and which is Sagittarius? And – according to the stars – which one of the boys is destined to be your true love?? Find out here . . .

Aston

Like other people born as an Aquarius, Aston has a lively and attractive personality. But underneath his cheeky exhibitionist exterior, lies a deep and sensitive soul. He is strong-willed and can usually see both sides of an argument, and is tolerant of other people's opinions, making him the JLS peacemaker. Like a typical Aquarius, Aston likes learning from other people, but he can sometimes be a loner. Aquarians are often gifted in the arts, music and drama, and work well in group projects – like being in the most awesome British boyband ever!

Some have gifts as entertainers and make good character actors (having an ability to mimic) and musicians. The more psychic among them possess healing gifts, especially in curing the mentally sick.

POSITIVE CHARACTER TRAITS OF PEOPLE BORN UNDER THE AQUARIUS SIGN:

- Friendly
- Honest and loyal
- Original and independent

AND NOT SO POSITIVE TRAITS:

- Argumentative
- Unpredictable
- Unemotional and detached

AQUARIANS LIKE:

- Fighting for good causes
- Dreaming and planning for the future
- Having fun

AQUARIANS DISLIKE:

- Being on their own too much

AQUARIUS – LOVE COMPATIBILITY!

Gemini, Libra and Sagittarius

These are matches made in heaven! All these three signs are sociable and like to have a lot of friends, but they also know when they need to have their own time. Some aspects of each other's personality might be annoying, but these signs can always forgive each other.

Aries, Aquarius, Virgo, Pisces and Leo

Hold onto your hat – these are stormy love connections! Sometimes Aries, Virgo and Leo can feel like they have different life goals from their desired Aquarius. But if both parties are willing to be patient with each other, it could turn into something special.

Taurus, Cancer, Capricorn and Scorpio

These are all strong signs, but Aquarians want to be free, and the other signs will find themselves wanting to dominate. Signs like Taurus, Cancer and Capricorn like routine and steadiness, while Aquarius is fun-loving and wants to run off to find new adventures. These signs just can't make a good romantic connection.

Marvin

Marvin is a typical Pisces. He has a gentle and patient nature and is generous and sensitive to other people's feelings. Pisceans get along with all kinds of people because of their easy-going nature. Pisceans like Marvin are good at accepting people around them, and because of their selflessness they often try to solve the problems of others rather than their own. Pisceans dislike convention and long to live creative lives; they aren't good at 9-5 jobs, and sometimes they can withdraw into a dream world.

Pisceans are also often creative and talented, and they love nothing more than to travel the world searching for new exotic places.

POSITIVE CHARACTER TRAITS OF PEOPLE BORN UNDER THE PISCES SIGN:

- Imaginative
- Sensitive
- Kind
- Sympathetic and selfless

AND NOT SO POSITIVE TRAITS:

- Secretive
- Vague
- Weak-willed and easily led astray

PISCEANS LIKE:

- Things that are ridiculous
- Getting lost and discovering new places
- Having their own time to daydream in

PISCEANS DISLIKE:

- Things that are obvious
- Being criticised
- People who are know-it-alls

PISCES – LOVE COMPATIBILITY!

Scorpio, Pisces and Cancer

With these signs matched to Pisces, it's usually a love at first sight situation! These three signs are noted for their jealousy, but that can make Pisceans feel like they're getting the attention and devotion they crave. These signs share a spiritual connection to Pisces, leading to a simply delightful bond.

Taurus, Virgo, Capricorn and Leo

Pisceans are affectionate and sincere creatures, and can make the lives of Taurus, Virgo, Capricorn or Leo full of joy. Pisces can be very emotional and can need stability and leadership in a relationship, which is something that these signs are good at providing.

Aries, Gemini, Libra, Sagittarius and Aquarius

Although there may be strong physical attraction between these signs and Pisces, unfortunately the connections end there. Pisces needs constant attention and devotion, and these signs can be too selfish to give up that much of themselves. The passion of these relationships will run high – but so will the problems.

SAGITTARIUS
SAGITTARIUS

JB and Oritsé

JB and Oritsé are both born under the Sagittarian sign, and as such, they share lots of the same character traits.

If there's one thing that JB and Oritsé have in common it's their positive outlook on life, which is typical of those born under the sign of Sagittarius. Sagittarians are very enterprising, they have a lot of energy and enjoy travelling and exploration. They are ambitious and optimistic, and when things don't go their way, they never let it get them down. JB and Oritsé are honest, trustworthy, loyal and generous, again typical character traits of those born under this sign.

Sagittarians love taking on new projects – perhaps one reason why JLS are so successful, and have a million projects on the go at any one time! Sagittarians like JB and Oritsé are strong-willed and good at organising, which means any project they undertake is almost always a success.

POSITIVE CHARACTER TRAITS OF PEOPLE BORN UNDER THE SAGITTARIUS SIGN:

- Optimistic
- Happy
- Freedom-loving
- Honest
- Intellectual

AND NOT SO POSITIVE TRAITS:

- Can be careless
- Irresponsible
- Superficial

SAGITTARIANS LIKE:

- Travelling
- Freedom
- Deeper meanings

SAGITTARIANS DISLIKE:

- Being constrained
- Having to be bothered with details

SAGITTARIUS – LOVE COMPATIBILITY!

Aries, Leo and Aquarius

These are usually ideal matches. Sagittarius is an active, spontaneous sign that likes socialising and enjoys the good things in life, as do Aries, Leo and Aquarius. While sometimes Sagittarians can be argumentative, the funny nature of these three signs will always bring a smile to the face. These are good signs that show compatibility physically, mentally and spiritually.

Gemini, Libra, Sagittarius, Capricon and Pisces

These signs are strongly attracted to Sagittarius. Affairs between them will probably begin impulsively, and are likely to be emotional rollercoasters. If they do end, they are likely to finish as abruptly as they started, but with a little effort from both sides, these could be love matches that last the distance.

Taurus, Cancer, Virgo and Scorpio

These are very different personality types from the Sagittarius. They can sometimes get angry with the Sagittarian's lofty ambitions and have different life goals from Sagittarius. Although they may feel happy in a relationship together, it is unlikely to last long. The passion of these relationships will run high – but so will the problems.

JLS Cupcakes!

If you're having some friends over, these special JLS cupcakes are just the thing you need. You can customise the colour of the icing depending on which boy is your favourite!

INGREDIENTS

FOR THE CUPCAKES

- 120g softened butter, cut into cubes
- 120g golden caster sugar
- 2 large eggs
- 125g self-raising flour
- 25g ground almonds
- ½ tsp vanilla or almond extract
- pinch of baking powder
- silver cupcake cases

FOR THE ICING

- 250g icing sugar
- Red, blue, green and yellow food colouring

INSTRUCTIONS – CUPCAKES

STEP 1 – Preheat the oven to 180C (or 160C if you have a fan assisted oven). Don't forget to get an adult to help you if you're not sure about using the oven. Then line a 12-hole cupcake tray with silver paper cases.

STEP 2 – Put the sugar, flour, butter, eggs and baking powder into a large bowl and mix together using an electric hand mixer for two minutes. The batter should be light and fluffy. Using a large metal spoon, mix in the ground almonds and vanilla extract.

STEP 3 – Spoon the mixture into the paper cases making sure you have an equal amount in each case. Bake for 20 minutes until the cupcakes rise. Leave in the tin for a couple of minutes, then lift the cakes onto a wire rack and leave until cold. Careful not to burn your fingers!

INSTRUCTIONS – ICING

STEP 1 – Stir about 2 tablespoons water into the icing sugar to give a smooth thickish paste. Split the mixture into four bowls and use a couple of drops of each food colouring in each bowl. You should then have four different coloured icings: red, blue, green and yellow.

STEP 2 – Spoon the different coloured icings over the cooled cakes so that the tops are almost covered and leave to set for a few minutes.

Then there's only one final step – sit down with your friends in front of a JLS video and get nomming on your special JLS cupcakes!

Code cracker!

Decipher the code and discover your secret JLS messages! Each letter has been replaced by a symbol, so use the guide and find out how you really feel. You can even use the symbols to write your own secret messages to the boys!

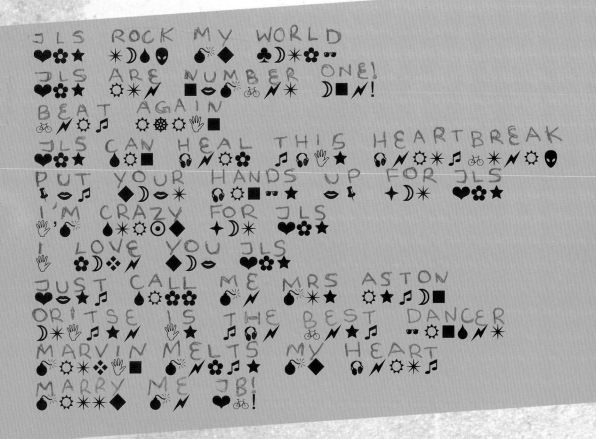

JLS ROCK MY WORLD

JLS ARE NUMBER ONE!

BEAT AGAIN

JLS CAN HEAL THIS HEARTBREAK

PUT YOUR HANDS UP FOR JLS

I'M CRAZY FOR JLS

I LOVE YOU JLS

JUST CALL ME MRS ASTON

ORITSE IS THE BEST DANCER

MARVIN MELTS MY HEART

MARRY ME JB!

GUIDE

a – ☼
b – 🚲
c – 💧
d – 👓
e – ⚡
f – ✦
g – ⚙

h – 🎧
i – ✋
j – 💙
k – 👽
l – ❀
m – 💣
n – ■

o – ☽
p – ⚓
q – ▲
r – ✳
s – ★
t – ♫
u – 👄

v – ❖
w – ♣
x – ☠
y – ◆
z – ◉

57

chapter 5

the future

With so many incredible demands on their time – collaborations with American superstars, a winter arena tour, the second album, the American market to conquer and a gritty urban BBC drama to star in – it doesn't seem possible they can achieve it all. But for these four humble lads from London, they've already done the impossible – and now, the sky's the limit!

The boys are really inspired to take their style back to the golden days of classic boy bands, keeping the all time greats like *NSYNC, Backstreet Boys and Take That in mind. 'When I first saw Justin [Timberlake] it was wicked. He was lifted above the fans on a crane. That inspired us to pull out all of the stops!'

Princess RiRi has already given them her endorsement. Like the rest of us, she's pretty keen on the boys. She's sure that under Jay-Z's wing, JLS could become the biggest group in the world. 'Under his management I think JLS will probably be the biggest,' says RiRi. 'They can sing, they can dance, they look good, actually they look very good.' Yes, they certainly do!

Fellow *X Factor* starlet, Leona Lewis also thinks JLS are in for big things. 'JLS are really representing,' she said. 'I think they'll do well in America – they could even be in the running for a Grammy.'

The boys have also got a wish list of people they'd like to work with – as well as RiRi, Jay-Z, Beyoncé and Kanye West! 'We're hopefully doing something with Taio Cruz,' says JB. Marvin would love the band to collaborate with Lily Allen, while Oritsé wants to work with the Backstreet Boys who were his heroes when he was growing up!

With so much planned, the boys have got a lot of work to do! 'Last year was mental,' says Marvin. 'We have a list of 300 goals. We need to keep the momentum going. There is so much we want to do.'

Luckily for them they're young, energetic, and have got all the passion they need. We'll be waiting for them to deliver the goods!

Picture Credits

All pictures courtesy of Getty Images.

Acknowledgements

Posy Edwards would like to thank Helia Phoenix, Viki Ottewill, Helen Ewing, James Martindale, Jane Sturrock, Nicola Crossley and Rich Carr.

First published in hardback in Great Britain in 2010 by Orion Books an imprint of the Orion Publishing Group Ltd.

Orion House, 5 Upper St Martin's Lane, London WC2H 9EA

An Hachette UK Company

10 9 8 7 6 5 4 3 2 1

A CIP catalogue record for this book is available from the British Library.

ISBN: 978 1 4 091 2311 8

Designed by Viki Ottewill

Printed in Italy by Rotolito

The Orion Publishing Group's policy is to use papers that are natural, renewable and recyclable and made from wood grown in sustainable forests. The logging and manufacturing processes are expected to conform to the environmental regulations of the country of origin. Every effort has been made to fulfil requirements with regard to reproducing copyright material.

The author and publisher will be glad to rectify any omissions at the earliest opportunity.

www.orionbooks.co.uk